Lizards

James Maclaine

Illustrated by Paul Parker

Additional illustrations by Becka Moor
Designed by Sam Whibley and Jenny Offley

Lizard consultant: Professor David Macdonald CBE,
Wildlife Conservation Research Unit, Zoology Department, University of Oxford
Reading consultant: Alison Kelly

Contents

The largest lizards are 100 times bigger than the smallest lizards.

Lizard world

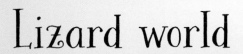

There are over 4,500 different types of lizards.

This lizard is a blue-nosed chameleon.

It lives in forests in Madagascar.

Warming up

All lizards have to keep themselves warm.

This rock gecko is resting
in a sunny spot to warm
its body.

If it gets too hot,
the lizard finds
somewhere in the
shade to cool down.

In some parts of the world, lizards go to sleep for several weeks or months when the weather is too cold.

A collared lizard digs a burrow under the ground.

The lizard goes into its burrow and sleeps there for the winter.

It wakes up in spring when it's warm again.

Scaly skin

Lizards have dry, scaly skin. Some lizards are smooth but others have bumps or spines.

This lizard is a thorny devil.

Animals won't try to eat it because of its sharp spines.

Most lizards shed their skin as they grow.

When a lizard is ready to shed, its skin starts to look dull.

The lizard rubs its body against rough rocks to loosen patches of skin.

It also rips off pieces of skin with its mouth. Sometimes it even eats them.

Some lizards puff out their eyes to shed skin from their eyelids.

Hungry lizards

Different lizards eat different types of food.

Caiman lizards eat snails but they spit out the shells.

Day geckos lick up a sweet liquid called nectar from flowers.

Many lizards eat insects which they swallow whole.

This land iguana is eating a type of cactus known as a prickly pear.

Tongue tricks

Lizards use their long tongues
to do lots of things.

This chameleon has caught
an insect to eat with the
sticky tip of its tongue.

A chameleon's tongue can
be twice as long as its body.

Monitor lizards flick out their tongues to taste different smells in the air.

A gecko licks its eyes clean. Most other lizards blink to clean their eyes.

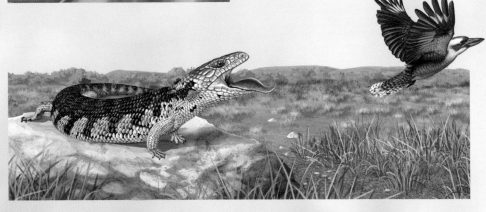

Lizards called skinks stick out their blue tongues to scare off other animals.

Life up high

There are lizards that live above
the ground in trees.

Some lizards can even move
through the air from one
tree to another.

This flying lizard
is using flaps of
thin skin to glide.

Lots of lizards are very good at climbing.

This green iguana is using its long toes and claws to climb up a tree trunk.

Geckos can climb upside down. Tiny hairs on their toes help them to grip.

Splash!

Lots of lizards spend time in water.
They can swim very well.

This marine iguana is sneezing
to remove salty seawater
from its body.

A green iguana dives into a river to escape danger.

It peeks out of the water to check if it's safe again.

Some lizards hunt in water.

This monitor lizard has caught a fish to eat.

Desert dwellers

Some lizards live in deserts where it's mostly dry and hot.

A web-footed gecko stays underground during the day.

It comes out as it starts to get dark and less hot.

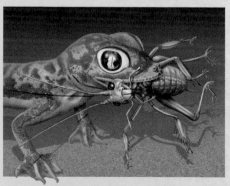

There are lots of insects awake at night for it to hunt.

This lizard is known as a sandfish.

It wriggles its body from side to side like a fish to move through the sand.

Desert iguanas get the water they need from the flowers they eat.

Blending in

Lizards often try to hide so dangerous animals can't find them easily.

There's a gecko hiding on this branch. Can you spot it?

Its skin and tail make it look like a leaf.

Some lizards change the way they look so the insects they hunt can't spot them.

A gecko finds a place to wait while it's hunting.

Soon, its skin turns darker to help it blend in.

Roundtail horned lizards make themselves look like rocks. They hunch up their bodies and tuck in their legs.

Escape artists

Sometimes lizards need to escape from animals that try to eat them.

A wall lizard can shed its tail if it needs to escape.

It takes several months for the lizard to grow a new tail.

This basilisk lizard is running over water to get away from danger. Skin between its toes stops it from sinking.

Lizards sometimes grow new tails that have more than one tip.

Keep back!

Lizards have lots of ways of staying safe.

A marine iguana whips its tail at a hawk that's trying to catch it.

An armadillo lizard holds its tail in its mouth to make itself into a spiny ball.

A horned lizard scares away a coyote by squirting blood from its eyes.

This frilled lizard has spread out flaps of skin around its head to make itself look big and scary. It's hissing too.

Showing off

Male lizards show off their bodies and make noises if they're trying to find female lizards.

A male chameleon is mostly green until he spots a female.

He then turns yellow and orange to attract the female.

This male fan-throated lizard has bright skin on his neck that attracts females.

If several male lizards find a female, they might fight. The strongest one will stay with her.

These Komodo dragons are wrestling to find out who is strongest.

Male tokay geckos make barking sounds to help females find them.

GEKK KAY GEKK

Laying eggs

Most types of lizards lay eggs.

This Chinese water dragon will leave her eggs after burying them in the ground.

Some lizards stay with their eggs until they hatch.

A mother skink wraps her body around her eggs to guard them.

If an egg feels cool, she picks it up with her mouth and puts it in a warm part of the nest.

Some lizards don't lay eggs. They give birth to baby lizards instead.

Baby lizards

Inside an egg, a baby lizard grows for several weeks or months.

When a baby is ready to hatch, it bites a hole through the shell of its egg.

The baby pokes its head through the hole. Then it pushes out its legs.

After it has hatched and had a rest, the baby digs its way out of the nest.

This is a baby male Pinocchio lizard.

Its nose
will get even
longer as it
grows up.

Glossary

Here are some of the words in this book you might not know. This page tells you what they mean.

 burrow - a hole in the ground where some lizards sleep or hide.

 shed - to lose a layer of skin or sometimes a tail.

 nectar - a sweet liquid made by flowers. Some lizards drink nectar.

 claw - a sharp nail. Most lizards have five claws on each foot.

 hunt - to search for, catch and kill animals to eat.

 hawk - a bird of prey. Some hawks try to catch lizards to eat.

 coyote - a type of wild dog. Coyotes eat some lizards.

Websites to visit

You can visit exciting websites to find out more about lizards. For links to sites with video clips and activities, go to the Usborne Quicklinks website at **www.usborne.com/quicklinks** and type in the keywords "**beginners lizards**".

Always ask an adult before using the internet and make sure you follow these basic rules:
1. Never give out personal information, such as your name, address, school or telephone number.
2. If a website asks you to type in your name or email address, check with an adult first.

The websites are regularly reviewed and the links at Usborne Quicklinks are updated. However, Usborne Publishing is not responsible and does not accept liability for the content or availability of any website other than its own. We recommend that children are supervised while on the internet.

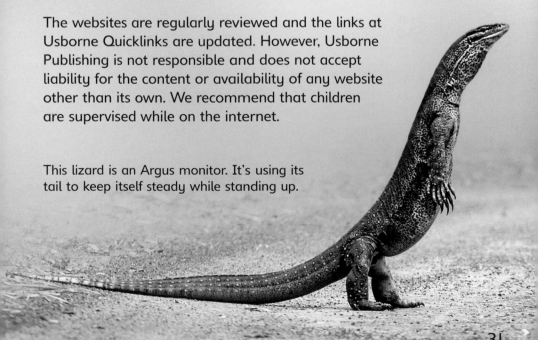

This lizard is an Argus monitor. It's using its tail to keep itself steady while standing up.

Index

Acknowledgements

Photographic manipulation by John Russell

Photo credits

The publishers are grateful to the following for permission to reproduce material: **Cover** © NaturePL/SuperStock; **p1** © kuritafsheen/gettyimages; **p2-3** © Minden Pictures/Alamy Stock Photo; **p4** © Fabio Pupin/FLPA; **p6** © Roger Laird; **p8** © Ann & Steve Toon/naturepl.com; **p9** © Tui De Roy/naturepl.com; **p10** © shikheigoh/gettyimages; **p12** © Ch'ien Lee/Minden Pictures/SuperStock; **p13** © John Cancalosi/naturepl.com; **p14** © Tui De Roy/Minden Pictures/SuperStock; **p15** © Barcroft Media/Contributor/gettyimages; **p17** © Chris Mattison/FLPA; **p18** © Thomas Marent/Minden Pictures/FLPA; **p20-21** © Bence Mate/naturepl.com; **p23** © Dwi Yulianto/EyeEm/gettyimages; **p24** © Arindam Bhattacharya/Alamy Stock Photo; **p25** © Andrey Gudkov/Alamy Stock Photo; **p26** © Placebo365/Dreamstime.com; **p29** © James Christensen/Minden Pictures/FLPA; **p31** © Sylvain Cordier/Biosphoto/FLPA

Every effort has been made to trace and acknowledge ownership of copyright. If any rights have been omitted, the publishers offer to rectify this in any subsequent editions following notification.

Sun, moon and stars

Farm animals

Elizabeth I

Rubbish & Recycling

Dogs

Horses and ponies

Spiders

Planes

Cats

Ancient Greeks

VOLCANOES

DINOSAURS

Your Body

Armour

Sharks

The Celts

VIKINGS

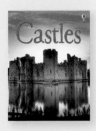
Castles

How flowers grow

Digging up the past

Living in space

Caterpillars and Butterflies

Ballet

Pirates

EGYPTIANS

Eggs and Chicks

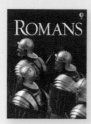
ROMANS

Weather

Tadpoles and Frogs

Why do we eat?

Under the Sea

Bears

AZTECS

TRUCKS

Night Animals

Firefighters

Antarctica

Bugs

COWBOYS

Planet Earth

London

Seashore

China

Dangerous Animals

Rainforests

Trees

Reptiles

Ships

Bats

Penguins